:)

"Tea Time is a
special time of Sharing!"

Sandra Hawk

Catering to Children

With Recipes for Memorable Tea Parties

CIRCA 1820

Heart to Heart books are available at a special discount for bulk purchases for fundraising efforts, sales promotions or educational use. Author available for speaking and book signings. Contact Heart to Heart Publishing for more information.

Printed in China.

Heart to Heart Publishing
519 Muddy Creek Road
Morgantown, Kentucky 42261
(888) 526-5589

Library of Congress Control Number: Applied for.
ISBN: 0-9742806-0-7

Heart to Heart Editor: Pearl Dexter
Heart to Heart Copy Editor: R. Elizabeth Doucet

Photographer: Barbara Yonts
(270) 821-2683

Layout and Design: Shelley R. Davidson
TreeMouse Design, e-mail: liltreemouse@aol.com

Contents

Introduction 4

Dedication 5

Preface 6

Hosting a Tea Party 9

Types of Teas 13

Serving Tea 17

Helpful Tea Etiquette Tips 21

Tea Party Games 25

Is Tea A Healthful Drink? 31

Tea History and Interesting Facts 33

Recipes 37

Savories 37

Pastries and Fillings 41

Cookies 44

Candies and Cakes 47

Definitions 53

Acknowledgements 55

Reference and Other Great Reading Sources 56

Introduction

Dear Friend of Children,

If you are one of those busy nine-to-five moms, or grandmothers wishing you were able to spend quality time with children, take courage. With help from this book, you can create wonderful memories.

My grandmother, Evelyn Webster, would bake tea cakes and serve them to me under a big shade tree. It was a simple setting upon a quilt, with summer breezes blowing. Whether I'm looking back to my childhood or the years of raising our sons, I realize that the times spent together fixing, mixing, or serving are some of my most treasured moments.

Dedication

*T*his book is dedicated with love to my best friend J.C. and my wonderful parents, Charlie and Mary Gill. They taught us the true meaning of the word *family*—it's about *how* we live, not *where* we live. May you laugh and grow closer while sharing this book from my family to yours—from my heart to yours.

—*L.J.H.*

*T*his book is dedicated to my grandmothers who gave me a love and appreciation for tea.

—*B.Y.*

Preface

My love for tea parties goes back to childhood days. My grandmother made the most delicious treats. One was tea cakes, simple, yet delicious. I looked forward to visiting and helping in her kitchen.

A spirit of genuine hospitality must prevail at an afternoon tea to make it a success, whether it is just having two or three friends together for an hour's chat or a large affair with many guests. It is heightened by bowls of flowers, lighted candles, beautiful dishes, attractive napkins, and finger foods daintily served with refreshing drinks. Games or entertainment may be added for everyone's pleasure.

I've enjoyed serving children tea from my antique tea sets, in my formal dining room, or outdoors in the flower garden. They were given instructions on conduct and proper manners and care of expensive items such as crystal, silver, and china. Of the many tea parties I've given, not one child has ever broken anything. We must teach children to appreciate the finer things in life, along with proper care for those things.

We can still recreate the atmosphere of a bygone era. I love the calming charm of a tea party with soft conversation, no rushing about, just taking time to enjoy each other's company.

The foods I most often serve are: finger sandwiches, fruit tray with crème-de-lite dip, a variety of desserts, and a selection of teas.

Hosting a Tea Party

Plan a comfortable setting for your tea party. I like to hear the grandfather clock ticking as soft music plays. In the winter we cozy up by the fireplace at a low table. Sometimes we have the perfect backdrop of winter, watching the snow gently falling into the goldfish pond beyond the big picture window.

In summertime we enjoy setting a round table with a starched tablecloth, near the pond and flower garden, and picking some of those flowers for our table. The sound of flowing water from the pond soothes my soul.

For an informal tea, I love to share tea at the kitchen table.

If it's to be a simple affair, keep the menu simple. Two kinds of finger sandwiches, scones, or a plate of small cookies and a dessert will do. Choose a tea to go with the food. Make the sandwiches into pretty shapes, using a cookie cutter or knife. Plan 3-4 small sandwiches per person. Have a variety of something sweet, sour, smooth, crunchy, or salty. Decorate the sandwiches for eye appeal. Never serve large sandwiches or desserts at teas; keep everything small.

Have soft music playing when the guests arrive. Greet them at the door, making them feel welcome. If you've prepared to play games, lead them into the game room until tea time. Have someone to help with games while you prepare the buffet and answer the door.

If you've arranged for entertainment, allow it to follow the tea, or begin when everyone has finished eating. During the performance, keep fresh tea available for the guests.

You may put a place cards where each guest sits. These may be made ahead of time. I use white or cream colored business cards printed with full name written in decorative script.

A nice addition is a special treat left beside each place setting. You could place exotic chocolates or hat cookies (see recipe in back of book) by each place setting.

When I prepare a large tea, each guest receives a program with the printed menu. I often include one of the recipes from the menu in the program.

For a small gathering, one person may do all the serving. For a large gathering, ask a friend or two to assist. Be sure to discuss details in advance as to your needs with preparation, presentation, and what foods will be served or passed around. Careful planning leads to a successful event.

If you're short on time and unable to prepare homemade recipes, consider purchasing quality foods from a gourmet shop and bakery. Children will still delight in the atmosphere you've lovingly created for them.

I always enjoy seeing girls and boys dressed up for tea parties. What young lady doesn't look pretty in a hat?

Sometimes we suggest that everyone bring his or her own cup and saucer to a tea party.

"*Take some more tea,*" the March Hare said to Alice.
"*I've had nothing yet,*" Alice replied in an offended tone,
"*so I can't take more.*"
"*You mean you can't take less,*" said the Hatter. "*It's very easy to take more than nothing.*"

— *Lewis Carroll*, Alice's Adventures in Wonderland *(1865)*

Types of Teas

Green

(Unoxidized) Best drunk without adding ingredients.

Oolong

(Partially Oxidized) Best drunk without adding ingredients.

Black

(Oxidized) May be enjoyed with milk, sugar, honey, or lemon.

Flavored

Teas have natural or artificial flavor added to the tea leaves; sometimes flower buds, and pieces of dried fruit.

Herbal

(Tisanes) "Teas" are not from the tea plant known as Camellia sinensis. They may be made from bark, roots, or flowers.

Making a Good Pot of Black Tea

Loose teas vary in size of the leaves; therefore, these instructions are for small, broken, black tea.

- Fill a tea kettle with freshly-drawn cold water, or use bottled water.
- Warm the teapot with hot water from the tap or from the kettle as it comes to a boil.
- Measure a 1/2 teaspoon of tea for each cup of tea.
- Add 1/2 cup boiling water for each cup (i.e. 3 cups of water for a 6-cup teapot). Return lid to teapot and let stand 3-5 minutes.
- Decant (strain) the tea into a second, warmed teapot all at once so that the tea will have the same taste for every cup served.
- The use of an infuser basket will omit the straining process into a second teapot.

Tea bags are convenient, with many flavors available. Be sure the water is boiling. Make the tea in a pot and remove the bags before you serve. If you use tea bags, do not squeeze them; which may add a bitter taste to the tea.

Making a Good Pot of Green or Oolong Tea

Because the size of the leaves differs so much from one green or oolong tea to another, we suggest that you follow directions for brewing from the package instructions. The water temperature required for brewing green and oolong teas is before the boiling point and may vary for the different teas. Pouring boiling water will burn the delicate leaves and may spoil the taste.

Iced Tea

Pour strong tea over cracked ice or ice cubes in glasses or a large pitcher. Add more ice. Tuck in sprigs of mint and slices of lemon or orange.

Serve very fine sugar, but not confectioner's, which would make the tea cloudy, as it contains cornstarch.

If so desired, add honey, artificial sweetenings, sugar cubes, milk, lemon or orange slices (1/2 inch slices, no wedges, with the seeds removed). Tuck a whole clove or two into each slice, if you wish. The citric acid of lemons will cause milk to curdle, therefore lemon and milk are never used together.

Serving Tea

*I*f you are serving tea for a number of guests, have a pot of strong tea and a pot of hot water on the tray so that you can serve as each one likes it, weak or strong.

You may serve from a tea wagon or a small table for just a few guests. At larger affairs (ten or more) you should have the table set and ask one or two friends to sit at each end to pour the tea and any other beverages.

The tea service is placed directly in front of the one serving, the plates to the left and the cups to the right. To avoid a cluttered look, no more than six to eight cups should be on the table at one time. The other foods, such as finger sandwiches, cakes, nuts, and candies, should be attractively arranged on serving pieces and placed on the table.

Being asked to serve tea is considered a great honor. After serving tea first, pass plates with sandwiches, scones, or small desserts. Always begin with the least sweet foods first.

The service may be buffet style, with the guests coming to the table for their drinks and helping themselves to the other foods, or the plates may be filled and passed to them. If there is a choice of drinks, guests should be asked their preferences. When tea is served, the accompaniments, lemon, milk, and sugar, should be added by the server.

Tea is always served by the host/hostess or someone appointed to do so. Tea is taken by the guest directly from the pourer.

The teacup and saucer should be in the left hand. Ask each person, "Do you prefer strong or weak tea?"

If the guest says, "Strong," pour the cup three-fourths full to prevent spills. Ask "Would you like milk, sugar, artificial sweetener, honey, or lemon?" Add the desired accompaniments.

If the guest says, "Weak," pour the cup only one-half full. This leaves space to add hot water for weak tea. Ask "Would you like milk, sugar, artificial sweetener, honey, or lemon?" Add these if desired.

Before handing the cup and saucer to the guest, lay a spoon on the saucer unless the guest requests plain tea (nothing is added). Then a spoon is not necessary.

Hot water is to remain upon the tea no longer than it takes to say Psalm 51 very leisurely.

– Sir Kenelm Digby

Helpful Tea Etiquette Tips

- Greet your guests at the door, and be sure to introduce them to guests who have already arrived.

- There should be no loud talking, running around, or boisterous games at a tea party.

- When seated at the table, place the napkin on your lap with it folded in half, having the fold toward your tummy with the top left corner folded down in a triangular shape. Only pat the inside of the fold on your lips when necessary. If you briefly leave the table, place the napkin on your chair. The host/hostess will not remove your plate, noting that you are to return. When the tea ends, simply place the napkin on the table (DO NOT re-fold it).

- Never use your own knife or fork to dip into butter, jams, and other condiments. Use only serving utensils.

- Do not reach across the table; ask for each item to be passed to you. Never point with a knife, fork or spoon while talking. Don't forget to say "please" and "thank you."

- Do not heap food onto plate. Take small bites.

- The proper way to eat a scone: gently break scone apart with a knife without cutting the scone. Next, place butter, jam, and clotted cream onto the edge of the plate; spread only enough butter, jam, and cream enough for one bite at a time. (Always spread butter first, jam second, and cream last.)

- Never place milk, lemon, or sweetening in cup before the tea.

- Never allow spoon to hit sides of the cup when stirring. Do not leave spoon standing in the cup; lay it across right side of saucer.

- Never fill cup to the brim. It is sure to spill.

- Sip your tea; no slurping.

- Always hold the cup with saucer when standing.

- Do not cradle the cup with your fingers.

- Look down into the cup while drinking. NEVER extend your pinkie finger while holding your cup.

- Do not talk about foods you dislike during a tea.

- When finished eating, place knife cutting edge toward you; lay fork across plate toward you. This signifies to host/hostess that you are finished.

- Do not push your plate back when finished eating.

- Always send your host/hostess a thank-you note.

Tea... that perfume that one drinks, that connecting hyphen.

– Natalie Clifford Barney,
Adventures of the Mind *(1929)*

Tea Party Games

$\mathcal{G}$ ames may be played while awaiting a tea. In earlier times, after a day with friends or family, all would gather in the parlor or library and play calm, simple games, or play-acting games, until time for the evening meal. At other times these games would be played after the meal. This was in wealthier homes where maids were preparing everything. If you plan games for your tea party, ask someone to help out.

I've Been Framed

This game is very simple, and any number of participants may play. It calls for self-control, which most players don't have at a party (especially, giggly little girls). Use a picture frame with the back removed. Holding it up in front of your face, you must present a still life picture, while all the others are making faces, calling you silly, but not rude or discourteous, names. Any player who lasts out the full minute as a still life picture should receive a suitable, small reward, perhaps a small mirror, or a Victorian picture frame.

Riddle-Me-Marie, I Spy

One player looks around room, spies an object that's visible to everyone in the room—a rosebud, let us say, and announces to the other players:

Riddle-Me-Marie, I spy something that you can't see and (give color) it is red. The other players then must guess what the object is. The first person with correct answer is allowed to "spy" the next object.

Taste

Before this game begins, set out and fill a number of glasses. Disposable are best. Use an assortment of beverages: hot tea (but not too hot), water, iced tea, vinegar, lemonade, milk, eggnog, and ginger ale. Each player is brought in one at a time, blindfolded. When reassured they will not be harmed in any way, they are then given a sip of each liquid. They must identify each one. The player who identifies the largest number of drinks is the winner. A winning prize could be a beautifully wrapped bottle of carbonated fruit juice or a variety pack of flavored teas.

Yes or No

This is a great game for getting people to communicate with others at parties. Each player is given five pennies. The players have to pair off and speak with each other. The aim is to trick the other player into using the words "yes or no." The first player will give a penny to the other who used the words "yes or no." The two players then split up and move on to new partners. The first player to get rid of all five pennies is the winner. A small prize is given.

Name It Game

This game may be played with two people, or two teams of any number or size group. Use flash cards (homemade or store bought) with letters A through Z. A score keeper has a one-minute timer. Another person shows the cards while the scorekeeper sets the timer. One card is shown to the "A" team. They must quickly name every word they can think of that begins with that letter, with only one minute to answer. Next the "B" team does the same. To make the game more difficult, each team must spell the word. Alternate from "A" team to "B" team until all cards have been used. This game makes you think and speak fast if you want to be the winner with the most words at the end of one minute. Total each team's words up when all cards have been used.

Drama Time

The group chooses one player to be the judge, and all others stand or sit in a row facing him or her. The judge commands them to express different emotions: guilt, anger, delight, joy, panic, despair, pride, enthusiasm, fear, happiness, sadness, etc. A small gift is awarded at the end for the player who has the most points for each emotion enacted.

The players should be allowed to use facial expressions, gestures, or speech, but to make it more difficult, they may be restricted to facial expressions only. Victorian women were known to express themselves dramatically.

Charades

Charades is a popular game in which one team of players has to guess a word or phrase the other team is acting out.

One group goes into a separate room and chooses a phrase or a word to act out. After deciding, they return to the other group to perform. The leader gives a small clue while players act out.

When the opposing team guesses correctly, they must leave the room and decide on a charade, returning to perform. If it cannot be guessed, the answer is supplied and the same team gets to perform again.

Card Games

Card games are great fun. Victorians often played cards. They are quiet games suitable for indoor tea parties. As a child, my favorite was *Old Maid*.

Is Tea A Healthful Drink?

Research focussing on the important contributions tea makes to our health is very promising. Studies suggest that four or more servings of green or black tea a day may have a positive impact on our health.

- Tea is the only drink known to stimulate, as well as soothe; it can perk you up in the morning and relax you in the evening.

- Tea is calorie free.

- Tea is a hydrator (helps maintain body fluid balance).

- Studies are showing that both green and black teas may reduce cancer risk of the skin, lungs, prostate, and breast.

- Five cups of tea have as many antioxidants as two fruits or vegetables.

- Studies are suggesting a link between tea and increased bone density.

- Tea may be beneficial against strokes and heart attacks.

- Tea has antibacterial properties that may help combat infections.

- Tea contains tannin (polyphenols) that may help cholesterol.

- Tea contains natural fluoride that may help prevent tooth decay.

Tea - it's for me. Something nice with a little spice.

– Linda J. Hawkins

Tea History and Interesting Facts

- Tea plants are evergreen bushes that have green serrated leaves with fragrant white blooms like wild roses. Its botanical name is *Camellia sinensis*, a distant cousin to the familiar camellia flower, *Camellia Japonica*, known in North America. Unpruned, the tea plant will grow into a tree 50 feet tall.

- The legendary discovery of tea was in 2737 B.C. by Chinese Emperor Shen-Nung. While he was sitting by a pot of boiling water, some leaves from a nearby tree fell into the pot. He enjoyed the resulting aroma and flavor the leaves gave to his drink. Thus the beverage of tea was born.

- The first published description of the tea tree and manner of making the beverage was c. 350 A.D.

- Dutch traders were the first to import tea from China to Europe c. 1610. It reached England around 1645 from Holland, at a dear price.

- The Dutch introduced tea to America when they settled in New Amsterdam (New York City) c.1650.

- When King Charles II of England married his Portuguese princess, Catherine of Braganza, in 1662, her dowry included three pounds of tea.

- During the mid-seventeenth century, ladies carried their own cups, saucers, and spoons, neatly tucked in a special pouch, to the evening teas.

- During the 1750s, tea gardens became popular in England. They served bread and butter with tea, and entertainment— poetry reading and strolling performers. It was a place to see and be seen.

- In 1773, tea was dumped into Boston Harbor from the English East India Company's consignment of tea because the colonists refused to pay the duty on tea that the English Parliament had imposed. Tea was also refused in Philadelphia and Charleston. New York, Greenwich, New Jersey, Annapolis and Chester Town, Maryland, and Edenton, North Carolina, either returned or dumped tea into the harbor. The captain of the *Peggy Stewart* was even forced to set fire to his ship in the port of Annapolis. In 1776, the American Revolutionary War resulted from the British attempt to enforce the tea duty without the colonists' consent.

- In the early nineteenth century, the Seventh Duchess of Bedford, Anna , started the trend of "afternoon tea." It has been written that Anna had a "sinking feeling" around five o'clock—she would order tea and cakes to stave off that feeling until the English customary late dinner.

- Iced tea was introduced in St. Louis during the 1904 World's Fair, when tea purveyor Robert Blechynden poured tea over ice. Today more than 90% of all tea consumed in the United States is iced.

- In 1908, New York importer Thomas Sullivan began sending samples of tea in small silk bags. Someone poured hot water over a bag, which began a revolutionary way to brew tea. In 1937, Faye Osborne invented tea-bag paper for the Dexter Corporation in Windsor Locks, Connecticut. They still supply a major portion of tea-bag paper throughout the world today. In the United States, the commonest way of brewing tea is with tea bags.

- South Carolina and Hawaii are the only two U.S. states where tea estates currently grow tea plants.

- Afternoon tea is a custom at Buckingham Palace. The Queen uses this time to spend with her family and pet corgis.

- Tea time is traditionally at four o'clock, but anytime between two and five o'clock is acceptable. Tea may be held in a cozy kitchen, a lovely garden, or an indoor, formal setting.

The tea hour is the hour of peace.... Strife is lost in the hissing of the kettle – a tranquilizing sound, second only to the purring of a cat.

– Agnes Repplier, To Think of Tea *(1932)*

Recipes

Savories

FESTIVE TEA SANDWICHES

1/2 cup salad dressing
2 Tbsp. finely chopped pecans
1/3 cup chopped cranberries
1/4 tsp. salt
1/8 tsp. pepper
16-24 thin slices sandwich-style chicken
   breast

Combine the first five ingredients and spread onto each slice of bread. Remove crusts. Layer the chicken onto bread cut into triangle shapes. Add a sprig of parsley to each top of bread; place one or two cranberries on the parsley.

CHILDREN'S FAVORITE SANDWICH

1 cup smooth or crunchy peanut butter
1/4 cup honey

Stir together until smooth, spread onto bread slices, trim crusts, and cut into 4-6 small pieces.

Note: Place a small crystal dish in center of crystal plate and fill with your choice of nuts. Arrange these peanut-honey sandwiches around nut dish.

Inkstands and tea-cups are never as full as when someone upsets them.

– Edith Wharton, A Backward Glance (1934)

CUCUMBER SANDWICHES

8 oz. cream cheese
1 Tbsp. dry Italian dressing mix

Mix until creamy and smooth; set aside. The flavor is enhanced when mixed 24 hours in advance.

1 large cucumber, thinly sliced, lightly salted, well drained.

Allow cucumber to sit one to two hours in colander. This is what makes a cucumber sandwich most suitable for eating, by preventing bread from becoming soggy.

WATERCRESS TEA SANDWICHES

8 oz. soft cream cheese
1/4 cup salad dressing
One or more bunches of fresh watercress

Remove hard stems from watercress, wash and drain. Mix the cream cheese and salad dressing until smooth. Spread soft cream cheese mix on bread; layer the watercress. Top with another slice of bread; trim crusts. Cut into decorative, petite shapes with cookie cutter or knife.

DELIGHTFUL HAM SANDWICHES

1 (4 1/2 oz.) can devilled ham
1/4 cup fat-free sour cream
2 Tbsp. sweet pickle relish, drained
1 Tbsp. grated onion
Dash hot pepper sauce

Mix all ingredients until well blended and smooth. Spread on bread slices; top with second bread slice. Trim crusts; cut into decorative, petite shapes with cookie cutter or knife.

Tip: Use both white and whole wheat bread to add contrast and options when making more than one kind of sandwich at a party. Decorate tops of sandwiches with olives, cherry tomatoes, and petite decorative-cut cheese slices.

Evening Tea is sweet to me,
just to be a friend with thee,
Each time we meet is such a treat.
An enchanted moment is this hour
bringing love such lofty power.

– Linda J. Hawkins

CHICKEN SALAD

1 - 4 lb. pkg. boneless chicken breast, boiled until chicken is completely cooked, then cool and chop.

Add:
1 cup salad dressing
1-1/2 cup sliced red grapes
1 cup Thousand Islands dressing
1 red apple, finely chopped
1/2 cup chopped pecans
2 Tbsp. pimientoes
4 Tbsp. sweet pickle relish

Wash and drain grapes and unpeeled apple. Combine all ingredients in a very large mixing bowl. Chill and serve on small croissants or bread slices cut into petite shapes.

MISS MARY'S PIMIENTO SPREAD

8 ozs. cream cheese
1 lb. Velveeta® cheese
1/3 cup chopped onion
4 oz. jar pimientos
1 cup salad dressing
3/4 cup sweet relish

Allow both cheeses to soften at room temperature. Place other four ingredients into blender and chop finely. Use a fork or potato masher to mix cheese with blended ingredients. Cut crust from bread; spread cheese on whole wheat bread. Cut into petite sandwiches.

PARTY CHEESE BALL

2 8 oz. packages cream cheese
2 tsp. Worcestershire sauce
2 cups (8 oz.) shredded mild cheddar cheese
1 Tbsp. chopped pimientoes
1 tsp. lemon juice
1 Tbsp. green pepper
1 Tbsp. onions
Finely chopped pecans or parsley as garnish

Combine softened cream cheese and cheddar cheese, mixing until well blended. Add pimientoes, green pepper, onion, Worcestershire sauce, lemon juice, and seasonings. Mix well. Chill. Shape into a ball. Roll in nuts or sprinkle with parsley. For a better blend of taste, mix one day ahead of party time.

TURKEY AND HAM ROLL-UPS

1 lb. package each of turkey and ham

Mix recipe for party cheese ball (page 39), lay meat out flat, spread with cheese mixture, roll from one end, and seal edge. Continue with other meats until all cheese mixture is used. Refrigerate roll-ups. Before serving, take out and cut into small pieces with sharp knife. Secure with decorative toothpick on a bed of lettuce with cherry tomatoes, olives, or cheese cubes.

HOT ARTICHOKE DIP

1 16 oz. can artichoke hearts
1/2 cup mayonnaise
1/2 cup drained plain yogurt
1 cup grated parmesan cheese
Dash of paprika

Drain artichoke hearts and mash well. Add remaining ingredients, mix with fork, and sprinkle with paprika on top. Bake in 350 degree oven for 30 minutes. Yield: 2 cups.

Note: This dip is also delicious served cold.

ZESTY ITALIAN DIP

3 cups low-fat yogurt
2 cucumbers, chopped
3 young green onions, finely chopped
1/2 tsp. basil
1/2 tsp. summer savory
1/4 cup chopped walnuts
1/4 cup sunflower seeds

Stir ingredients and chill. Serve with vegetables cut small or crackers.

SPICY MINI-SMOKIES

2 pkgs. Little Smokies®
2 cups barbecue sauce (I prefer smoked)
1 cup grape jelly

Mix jelly and BBQ sauce until smooth, pour into crockpot, and add Little Smokies. Cook on high 2-3 hours, turn down, and keep warm until serving time. This recipe may be easily doubled for a large group.

Pastries and Fillings

SIMPLE TEA ROOM SCONES

3 cups self-rising flour
1/2 cup sugar
1 stick butter
1 cup buttermilk

Prepare as you would biscuits; handle gently, cut into shapes, or leave round. I prefer a heart-shaped cutter. Bake at 400 degrees.

For variations add: 1 tsp. cinnamon and 1/2 cup raisins; chocolate chips and 2 Tbsp. cocoa; or 2 Tbsp. poppy seed and 1 Tbsp. lemon zest; or top with one of the following:

RASPBERRY BUTTER

1 stick sweet cream butter (no margarine or substitutes)
3 Tbsp. raspberry preserves

Allow butter to soften to room temperature. Stir preserves into butter. Place in crystal covered dish; serve with scones or hot biscuits. May also place in butter mold. Refrigerate until firm and un-mold when ready to serve.

HONEY BUTTER

1 stick sweet cream butter (no margarine or substitutes)
1 Tbsp. honey

Allow butter to soften to room temperature. Stir honey into butter until smoothly mixed. Serve with freshly-baked goods.

MICROWAVE LEMON CURD

3 eggs
1/2 cup fresh or bottled lemon juice
1 stick butter, melted
1 cup sugar

Beat eggs in a glass bowl. Stir in lemon juice, sugar, and melted butter. Microwave on high for three minutes. Remove and stir with a wire whisk. Microwave again for three minutes, whisk again. Repeat if necessary. Don't forget the mixture will thicken when it cools.

GLAZED PETITE PASTRY

1/4 cups sour cream at room temperature
1 pkg. dry yeast
1 large egg, lightly beaten
1 cup softened butter
2 cups all purpose flour
1 cup fruit preserves, your choice

Glaze:
1 cup powdered sugar
2 Tbsp. milk
1/2 tsp.vanilla

Heat oven to 400 degrees. Combine sour cream and yeast. Set aside 10 minutes. Stir in egg. Set aside. Cut butter into flour. Stir in sour cream until dough comes together. On a lightly-floured surface, roll out dough to 1/4 inch thick. Cut into 2 1/2-inch rounds. Transfer to ungreased cookie sheets. Cover with towel for 15 minutes. Make a thumbprint in the center of each cookie. Fill with 1/2 tsp. preserves. Bake 12-15 minutes. Drizzle with sugar glaze.

MELON-BERRY DIP

Fresh strawberries, peach or melon slices
1 8 oz. tub whipped topping, thawed
1 Tbsp. grated orange peel
1/2 cup crushed strawberries
1 8 oz. container strawberry low-fat yogurt

Wash fruit, slice or cube, set aside. Mix half the whipped topping and orange peel in small bowl. Mix whipped topping, crushed strawberries, and yogurt in separate bowl. Dip whole strawberries, sliced peaches, and melon cubes into mixture. Serve with decorative toothpicks.

Note: Store any leftover dip in refrigerator. This is a summer refresher served in the outdoor garden setting for evening tea.

CRÈME-DE-LITE FRUIT DIP

1 8 oz. pkg. fat-free cream cheese, softened
1 tsp. vanilla flavoring
1/2 tsp. almond flavoring
8 Tbsp. skim milk
16 pkgs. artificial sweetener or 1/2 c. powdered sugar
1 cup fat-free whipped topping

Allow cream cheese to soften, then mix with all other ingredients. Serve immediately or chill. Will keep in refrigerator up to one week. Wash, scrub, and slice red and green apples, kiwi, bananas, oranges, grapes, and strawberries. Arrange on large tray in a attractive manner, with dip in the center.

Note: Before placing on tray, dip apples and bananas in 2 cups cold water mixed with 4 Tbsp. lemon juice. This will keep them from turning dark and not affect taste of fruit.

Variation: 8 oz. any flavor yogurt, omitting vanilla and almond flavorings.

Pineapple dip: Omit skim milk; and substitute pineapple juice instead. Chopped pineapple optional.

Cookies

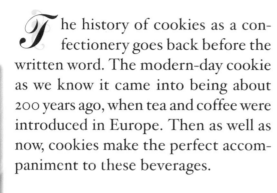

The history of cookies as a confectionery goes back before the written word. The modern-day cookie as we know it came into being about 200 years ago, when tea and coffee were introduced in Europe. Then as well as now, cookies make the perfect accompaniment to these beverages.

ALMOND COOKIES

1/2 cup powdered sugar
1 cup flaked almonds
1/2 cup all-purpose flour
3/4 cup butter
1 tsp. fresh lemon juice
1 egg

Preheat the oven to 375 degrees. In a large mixing bowl, mix butter and sugar until light and fluffy. Add the flaked almonds to the mixture. Mix well. Add the lemon juice and the egg. When this is well-blended, add the flour a little at a time. Make sure all these ingredients are thoroughly mixed. Roll teaspoonfuls of dough into balls (or use a cookie press). Place 2 inches apart on an ungreased cookie sheet. Bake at 375 degrees for 10-15 minutes. Cool on wire racks. Makes 5 1/2 dozen cookies.

CHOCOLATE THUMBPRINT COOKIES

1/2 cup (1 stick) butter, softened
1 cup flour
2/3 cup sugar
1/3 cup cocoa
1 egg yolk
2 Tbsp. milk
1 cup flour
Pecans or chocolate chips
1 tsp. vanilla extract

Soften butter in microwave for 1 minute. Add sugar, milk, egg yolk, and vanilla. Beat with large spoon or spatula; add flour and cocoa. Beat until smooth. Refrigerate 1 hour or more until firm. Spray cookie sheet. Heat oven to 350 degrees. Roll dough into one inch balls and place on cookie sheet. Push thumb into center and place a pecan or chocolate chips into thumbprint. Bake 10-12 minutes. Allow to cool 2-3 minutes in pan, then move to wire rack until completely cool. This is for chocolate lovers, large and small.

HAT COOKIES

This recipe makes a beautiful decoration for each guest to take home.

18-24 sugar cookies 2 1/2 -3-inches
    across
18-24 large marshmallows
2 lbs. powdered sugar
1/2 cup light corn syrup
1 tsp. vanilla
1/2 cup hot water
Food coloring, added last, soft pastel
    colors for spring and summer, darker
    colors for fall and winter.
Decorative small flowers, feathers, or
    ribbons

Mix well sugar, corn syrup, vanilla, hot water, and food coloring. If too stiff heat a *few seconds* in the microwave. When desired density colors are

achieved, place a tray under wire racks. Put cookies on top rack with a marshmallow on top at each, pour icing over each cookie and marshmallow hat; decorate while still wet with flowers, ribbons or feathers, allow several hours to dry and harden. Icing in tray may be melted for re-use. Place one hat upon a paper doily beside each place setting. The smiles of delight will repay you for your efforts.

Note: Desired density is sometimes hard to achieve because stirring is required.

COOKIE KISS

1 roll chocolate chip cookie dough
1 bag chocolate kisses

Spray mini-muffin tin with cooking spray. Preheat oven to 350 degrees. Slice cookie dough, then cut into fourths and place one fourth into each muffin tin. Smooth out and add one unwrapped kiss to center of each dough. Bake until cookie edges are brown.

TEA TASSIES

1 cup flour
1 stick butter
1 3 oz. pkg. cream cheese

Filling:
1 large egg
2 Tbsp. melted butter
1 cup brown sugar
1 cup finely chopped pecans

To make tarts, mix all ingredients to make pastry. Chill. Form small tarts in tart pan. Mix all ingredients together and fill tart shells. Bake at 350 degrees for 20 minutes.

Candies and Cakes

DELIGHTFUL DIVINITY

2 1/2 cup sugar
1/2 cup light corn syrup
1/2 cup water
1 tsp. vanilla
2 egg whites
Dash of salt

Combine sugar, syrup, water, and salt in pan. Bring to a boil, stirring constantly. Boil until mixture reaches 260 degrees on candy thermometer. While the above cooks, beat egg whites until stiff in large glass mixing bowl. Gradually add syrup mixture to egg whites, continuing beating while pouring. Add vanilla flavoring. Beat until mixture is thick enough to drop by teaspoonsful onto waxed paper. To make more attractive, place a walnut or pecan half on top of each. Serve in foil mini candy cups.

NUTTY PEANUT BUTTER FUDGE

6 cups sugar
3 sticks butter
1 can evaporated milk
1 pint crunchy peanut butter (or smooth peanut butter, for smooth and creamy fudge)
1 Tbsp. vanilla
13 ozs. marshmallow cream

Mix first three ingredients together. Bring to a rapid boil, stirring constantly. Boil 12 minutes. Remove from heat, add marshmallow cream, and vanilla, then peanut butter. Stir until all is smooth and melted. Pour into large cake pan or cookie sheet; let cool and cut into squares. This makes 5 pounds.

ORANGE DREAMSICLE FUDGE

3/4 cup butter (not margarine) – reserve
   1/2 tsp. butter to grease 9"x13" pan
3 cups. sugar
3/4 cup whipping cream

Boil butter, sugar, and cream ingredients for 4 minutes.

Add:
10 -12 oz. bag white vanilla chips
7 oz. marshmallow cream

Mix until melted. Pour into 9" x13" pan. Set aside. Reserve one cup vanilla mixture.

Add to the larger mixture:
3 tsps. orange extract
12 drops yellow food coloring
5 drops red food coloring

Blend well. Swirl 1 cup vanilla mixture into the pan of orange candy. Cool. Cut into small squares. Yields 2 1/2 pounds.

CREAMY CHOCOLATE FUDGE

6 cups sugar
3 sticks butter
1 can evaporated milk
2 12 oz pkgs. chocolate chips
1 Tbsp. vanilla
13 ozs. marshmallow cream

Mix first three ingredients together. Bring to a rapid boil, stirring constantly. Boil 10 minutes. Remove from heat, add marshmallow cream and vanilla. Add chocolate chips. Stir until all is smooth and melted. Pour into large cake pan or cookie sheet. Let cool and cut into squares. Makes 5 pounds.

KENTUCKY BUCKEYES

1 1 lb. box confectioner'ssugar
1 tsp. vanilla
1 stick butter, softened at room temperature, not in microwave
1 12 oz pkg. semi-sweet chocolate chips
1 cup peanut butter
6 Tbsp. paraffin

Mix sugar and butter. Blend in peanut butter and vanilla until smooth. Chill, then roll into small balls. Melt chocolate and paraffin. Dip balls into melted chocolate. Allow them to cool completely. Store in refrigerator.

Victorian Bonnet Cake

1 1/2 boxes yellow cake mix (I use butter recipe)
1 cup water
1 1/2 sticks butter
4 eggs.

Beat per package instructions. Grease and flour a 12" pan for hat brim and 1 1/2 quart oven proof bowl for crown of hat. Pour 2 1/2 cups of batter in bowl and remaining batter in pan. Bake at 350 degrees, pan for 20 to 30 minutes, the bowl for 30-40 minutes, checking every few minutes. When done turn out on wire rack to cool.

Buttercream Icing
1 1/2 cup solid Crisco
1 1/2 tsps clear vanilla
3/4 tsp butter flavoring
3/4 tsps almond flavoring
3 Tbsps water
6 cups sifted confectioners sugar

Cream shortening with electric mixer, add flavorings and mix, add confectioners sugar gradually beating well after each addition. Icing will be dry, add water 1 tablespoon at a time until icing is light and fluffy. Place 2 1/2 cups of icing into small bowl. Add pink food coloring to make pretty pink icing for trim. With remaining icing add yellow food coloring to make light yellow color.

Spread yellow icing on top of hat brim, place crown of hat in center, cover all with yellow icing and smooth. Using a cake decorating bag and decorator tip #70 make ruffle around brim of hat with tip #2B make ruffle around base of hat crown.

Let dry and decorate with silk flowers and ribbon. Icing colors, flower and ribbon can be colors of your choosing.

If you are cold, tea will warm you. If you are heated, it will cool you. If you are depressed, it will cheer you. If you are excited it will calm you.

– *William Ewart Gladstone*
(1809-1898)

*There are few hours in life
more agreeable than the hour
dedicated to the ceremony
known as afternoon tea.*

– Henry James (1843-1916)

Definitions

afternoon tea: Considered a four-course menu, the first serving is usually finger sandwiches. Scones, sweets, desserts, and choice of tea to follow. It may also be as simple as a piece of toast and a cup of tea

à la carte: A separate price for each item on the menu (the case in many tea houses)

clotted cream: A dense cream with a butter consistency.

crumpet: A batter cake heated on a griddle and usually toasted before serving with butter and jam.

elevenses: An English custom equal to the American "coffee break"; tea is served.

etiquette: The proper use of good manners; sometimes called social graces.

high tea: An afternoon or evening meal composed of savories: meats, fish, fowl, meat pies, quiches, cheese, relishes, fruits, and a variety of desserts, at which tea, of course, is the beverage. It is sometimes served buffet style, and often confused with Afternoon Tea.

infuser: A basket that holds loose tea leaves for brewing

mincemeat: A mixture of marmalade, apples, nuts, sugar, candied peel, raisins, and spices. It gets better with age when stored in airtight jars.

pastry: Flour dough made with shortening for pie crust, tarts etc., all fancy baked goods.

royal tea: The same as Afternoon Tea, with the addition of champagne or sherry; you may serve non-alcoholic drinks such as punch, or flavored mineral water to create one's own Royal Tea for children.

savories: A small, highly seasoned portion of food served, such as finger foods

scone: Often referred to as beautiful bread, a tea cake resembling a baking-powder biscuit. Usually served with jam and clotted cream.

sultana: A small white, seedless grape or raisin used in baking desserts

welsh rabbit: (A humorous usage) Cheese, often mixed with ale, served on crackers or toast. The correct name is Welsh rarebit.

Acknowledgements

A book is never the work of one person. It takes many people working together to achieve the desired results. I once heard someone say, "If you see a turtle on a fencepost, be assured he didn't get there alone. Someone put him there." I gratefully acknowledge each person God has placed in my life to see this book through to completion. I didn't get here by myself.

Thanks to Ray Hawkins, my number one supporter and the love of my life for the last thirty years.

Thank you to photographer Barbara Yonts for her excellent work, editor Pearl Dexter and copy editor R. Elizabeth Doucet for their hard work and patience; to Shelley R. Davidson, designer – great job.

Thanks to helpful support from Butler County Library Staff – Sibyl, Kenna, Connie, Lorie, Joyce, and Mary.

Thanks to these helpful people: Kathy of Central City Corner Fashions; Bruce, Denise, Brenda, April L., Evelyn, Angel, Pat, Bea, Patty, and Ramona.

Thanks to recipe helpers Ruby, April L., April P., Joan, and Mary.

Thanks to the following homeowners for allowing photo shoots at their residence: Roy Gill, Russellville, KY; Mary Hampton, Morgantown, KY; Michelle Wester, Rochester, KY; Mary Defini, Donald Bowles I, and Barbie Hunt, all of Madisonville, KY.

Thanks to all the models:

Abby	Dixie	Katie	Samantha P.
Addie	Faith H.	Kaylee	Sarah
Alexis	Faith Y.	Keely	Savannah
Aly	Grahmn	Laura	Shayla
Angela	Hannah	Lauren	Trevor
Barbie	Heather D.	Macy	Wes
Ben	Heather G.	Matthew	Zachary
Braydee	Jenna	Michael	Zoic
Chandler	Jessica	Rachel	
Chelsea	Jett	Ryan	
Claire	Kasidy	Ryder	
Daniel	Kately	Samantha G.	

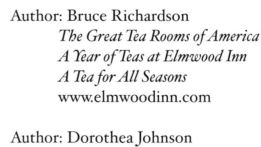

Reference and Other Great Reading Sources

Author: Bruce Richardson
    The Great Tea Rooms of America
    A Year of Teas at Elmwood Inn
    A Tea for All Seasons
    www.elmwoodinn.com

Author: Dorothea Johnson
    Tea & Etiquette

Author: Letitia Baldrige
    Complete Guide to the Manners for the 90's

Author: Emily Post
    Emily Post's Etiquette

Tea: A Magazine®
    www.teamag.com
    (888) 456-8651